Angles of Departure

Angles of Departure

Poems by Marcene Gandolfo

Cherry Grove Collections

Published by Cherry Grove Collections
P.O. Box 541106
Cincinnati, OH 45254-1106

ISBN: 9781625490650
LCCN: 2013957795

Poetry Editor: Kevin Walzer
Business Editor: Lori Jareo

Visit us on the web at www.cherry-grove.com

Acknowledgments

I gratefully acknowledge the editors of the following publications, where these poems, sometimes in slightly different forms, have appeared:

Bayou: "Anamnesis"

The Café Review: "Field"

California Quarterly: "Stitches," "There"

DMQ Review: "Missed"

Earth's Daughters: "The Dance"

Eclipse: "Found," "Reprise"

Francis and Claire in Poetry: An Anthology: "Transubstantiation"

Georgetown Review: "Potion"

Harpur Palate: "The Flames," "A Tide"

Inertia: "Hold," "In December"

Inkwell: "Listen" (published as "Suburban Numb")

Late Peaches: Poems by Sacramento Poets: "The Night Held Them," "Summer after His Death" (reprint)

Meridian Anthology of Contemporary Poetry: "Lost" (long version, reprint), "Why"

Mezzo Cammin: "Taking Down the Crib"

Paterson Literary Review: "Migration"

Poet Lore: "Lost"

Red Rock Review: "Because He Feared the Call to Vietnam" (published as "Storm")

Red Wheelbarrow: "Lost" (long version, reprint)

River Oak Review: "Dream in a Forgotten Language"

Sow's Ear Poetry Review: "Estate Sale"

Van Gogh's Ear: "Summer after His Death"

I would also like to express my sincerest gratitude to all those who have helped me through the process of creating this book.

For their generous insights and feedback, I offer special thanks to Sandra Alcosser, Marvin Bell, Kwame Dawes, Diane di Prima, Molly Fisk, Susan Kelly-DeWitt, and Timothy Liu.

Thanks also go to Michelle Bitting, Gale Hemmann, Jeanne Morel, and Robert Peake, for their motivation and support, and to Diane di Prima's Theory and Practice of Poetics class, for inspiring me to begin this project.

I also thank Shelley Washburn and the Master of Arts in Writing program at Pacific University.

My love and gratitude go to Tom and Marissa—for their endless support and encouragement.

I would like to express my gratitude to Martha Carlson-Bradley, for her thoughtful and generous editing skills.

And finally, many thanks to Kevin Walzer and Lori Jareo, for selecting and publishing this book.

Contents

I

II

III

I

For our house is our corner of the world. It has been said,
it is our first universe, a real cosmos in every sense of the word.

The point of departure of my reflections is the following:
every corner in a house, every angle in a room,
every inch of secluded space in which we like to hide,
or withdraw into ourselves, is a symbol of solitude for the imagination:
that is to say, it is the germ of a room, or of a house.

—Gaston Bachelard

Anamnesis

My summerhouse is empty now. You may know the house. I built it one night in a sugared dream. The lights are always on and the oven bakes cookies. The backyard trees blossom but fruit never ripens and the sweet-toothed child eats strawberries and dances to a scratchy phonograph song no one has heard before. But one night, the music stops. I wake. The doctor says no heartbeat and I see the child is only a folded cloud on an ultrasound. Then I say my summerhouse is empty now. It lives in a town I didn't enter because of bad weather. It stands on a street never crossed. Yet some days when I see my beveled face in a mirror, again I enter that full summerhouse. I hear its music in the sound of tumbling water and the music is yours too. That's when I say come in. Because nothing remains empty. Come in. Listen with me and we will hear the phonograph play the song that was lost before we were born.

Lost

The summer after the baby died, I tried to keep the cat alive, her old
kidneys closing. The only remedy was water.

That's all I remember that summer, saline bags hanging from the wall,
the faithful drip of the needle, my hands

steady as I pinched her skin and pushed the needle under her shoulder,
where she would lie against my swollen belly and purr

as her hollow body filled again with hunger and she would dance young
for an hour and then moan for more water. That's all

I remember that summer. Hanging those bags of water, breaking open
a new needle, finding the proper angle, the pinch and the push,

the push and the skin breaking and some days water spilling over
my knuckle, some days a drop of blood on my thumb

and the pushing and the dripping until one day the cat stopped crying
for water and only wanted to sleep

and the bag of saline was a folded lung on the wall.

*

Now I walk in the forgotten garden. I am bare feet on weeds
in this garden

where everything has gone overgrown and yellow, except
one rosebush that lives against the fence.

A jagged line of water from a neighbor's broken sprinkler running
under green leaves and three roses, opening. I want

to smash them down with my hands because I know the sun will singe
them white in less than a week. But then I watch

their violet petals pushing upward, releasing as a clenched fist opens
after the fight is over and I leave them

still pushing into that afternoon, dissolving into sun.

Why

here
where the orchard
ends

burnt
twigs smolder above
the white

farmhouse
where a woman
breaks

eggs
in her kitchen
window

tell me
why do you
feel

cold
yolks slide
over

your
own chapped
hands

If

it happened once, it will happen again, she said, as she stood outside her house near the singing river. She remembered the day the great redwood fell from the mountain and split the town center. For weeks, the others fixed roads, hammered buildings. They paved a new footbridge over the fallen tree. They kept the tree there as a relic of error, a reflection of their own slips and tears. They offered to walk her across. She refused. She stood outside her house near the singing river and shook her head, *If it happened once, it will happen again.* Everyone grew older. Her hair turned silver. She took to knitting colorful sweaters. In the morning, as the others walked toward town, they watched her rocking in the porch swing, singing with the river, knitting, a piece of yarn tethered to the basket at her bare feet. Now she rarely noticed them. Her hands too busy knitting to wave. Her voice too melodic to say see you later. When they crossed the footbridge, they thought of their insignificant failures. And as they heard thunder over the redwood mountain, they knew she was right. If it happened once, it would happen again. Still, each morning they crossed. Each morning they stepped ahead. They made their choices. They took their chances.

Found

Eight p.m. October night. Clean
plates placed into the dark
cupboard. A reflection
in a toaster reveals
a part of you—
missing.

As when your daughter breaks
into laughter and her smile
displays a dark gap
where the tooth
once took its place.

Or when a woman reading
on a train travels so deeply
into story she forgets
the wristwatch ticking
to her pulse. As people swarm
the doors, exit the last
station, she has lost her destination.

Outside your window, above
the sidewalk, a stream of cat
eyes lights the night sky—
searching.

Sparrows

I walked in circles
for miles

and the circles grew closer
together.

Each time I turned, sparrows
grew closer

with singing. Then I could
hear the feathered

air shake the earth.

*

All day I drew sparrows
with blue feathers

on my kitchen table. My wrist spun
them in circles.

My pencil shook. I began
to sing.

The sparrows
landed

at my window. My song rang
through

a crack in the glass.

Reprise

When the music comes back,
it wakes you. When the music
comes back, it takes the shape
of a bride beneath a streetlight.
And as you say *yes,* your body
wants to sing again, remember
a constellation of notes: the voice
that made the plate glass tremble,
the one that turned to blood.

In December

It was the day for origami,
the day I taught my daughter to fold
a perfect five-point star,

not cut, tear or paste
but feel each paper square
as a body, see its scars

and creases against our own,
fold corner-to-corner, fraction
upon fraction, fold flat then

open, unfurl a new
sum, unearth an answer
in the shell of it.

When we finished folding
I couldn't tell her it happened again.
I couldn't say, *No baby*

in May. I could only
carry the paper constellation,
like shards of some

heavenly wreckage, to the tree
luminous with silver bulbs and golden
angels. I could place stars

against the pine needles. I could
stand in the vertigo of flickering light.
Light that shattered through

our translucent stars. Light
that ricocheted to the wood-stained

manger, to the pallid faces

of three wise men
who overlooked the porcelain infant
that lay so still.

Hold

The face that was tomorrow becomes today. It takes its shape: one day an ashen moon, the next, a beveled oval. In morning dust, see it congeal; see it outside your door in the porch light as you stoop to your newspaper. Why do you turn your head and close the door?

Once I saw the most doll-faced girl. Porcelain skinned, apple cheeked and voiceless as her mother threw her against the supermarket wall. And I, a child myself, watched the girl hold her face without flinch or tear as she fell to the ground. She lay silent as a stack of paper towels fell over her rigid body. Then a butcher with a bloodstained apron lifted the doll-girl to her feet. And everyone stood quiet as she ran out the door, to follow her mother.

Last night, I dreamed you reached for me in a room full of chiming clocks. I felt a veil of skin fall from my face. Then you were gone, and I was alone, only one clock striking in the corner. I walked to it. I saw my reflection in the glass of its face.

If you stare at anything long enough, you will see its face. See the profile in the door before you. See its features take shape in the grain.

The face that was tomorrow becomes today. One day a wing of fog, one day a button of dust. Why do you turn away? If I were wise, I would tell you to do what I can't. If I were wise, I would tell you to embrace it like a lover, taste the salt in its breath, and listen, even if its teeth gnash in your ear.

When

A man's watch stopped at three minutes to twelve. He didn't know why
or where . . .

Was he picking up lunch? Was he swatting a fly? Was he
at a stoplight,

staring at an abandoned building where children etched their names
into an icy window?

The light turned green. The jeweler shook his head and said, *This isn't
worth fixing.*

These things happen, he sighed. And the alphabet on the window
turned to water. The man writhed

the watch from his arm, stared at two poised hands, three minutes
to twelve, palms nearly together

in mechanical prayer, through the round, naked window. On his wrist
a chafed line

like a whisker beneath the skin, the same mark he saw on his father
the day he took the watch, the ring, from the pale body.

The man forgot to buy a new watch the next day
and the next.

He found so much beyond the spectacle of time. He knew
when noon stabbed

through his office window. He could feel the calm salt of evening settle
against his skin.

He could kiss the infant wrist of midnight like the wrist of his daughter the day she was born.

From the Margin

I'm looking through the absence
of the field.

All day it is with me, the way
every absence is

a presence. I have no memory
of the word

I want to utter, only that it's a word
in a language

not yet invented. I think
I can see

the unborn world contemplate
itself beneath

the white grass. Today
I think I see

my unborn son run into the absent
field.

He turns to say, *Stay back.*
This is my white grass.

Taking Down the Crib

You turn the metric wrench until each rivet
falls to carpet and place each unused piece
into the wooden box. We feel the weight
and carry it away. Now just a press
against the rug, a smudge of dust, no stain
too great to be erased. Except one streak
of light across the wall. It must have been
a sunbeam through the window, against bleak
blue paint. It bleached a line white. It's best
not to ask questions of what can't be explained
so I'll pull the blinds, close the door, won't guess
why this light shone, why another waned
in the house where we pretend to forget
in the empty room where no child slept.

Dream in a Forgotten Language

That the word had never broken
against the sea rock, its own peculiar

letters shattered. Pieces of shells
remain in our wake, *explain composition*

and time above the calm. Here we
configure a new language, *beginning again*

and again, but where, in the body
does this longing arise? Beyond the shore

on a ship's deck, a man and woman
open the urn that holds their infant's ashes.

Today they will learn this is not letting go
as ashes fall from the wind against their dark

suits, *beginning again and again.* What they give
will return, always in a slight and broken grain

always the color of dust.

II

*The city does not tell its past, but contains it like the lines
of a hand, written in the corners of streets, the gratings of windows,
the banisters of the steps, the antennae of the lightning rods,
the poles of flags, every segment marked in turn
with scratches, indentations, scrolls.*

*The city exists and it has a simple secret: it knows only departures,
not returns.*

—Italo Calvino

Letter Unsent

1

It began before our parents stopped speaking, our eleventh
summer of cotton dresses, lemonade and stale

radio songs. It began the summer we drew our perfect city
from a box of colored chalk.

On your patio, I opened my left hand down to the dirty cement
as my right turned powdery lines,

drawing streets until darkness erased them. Each day
we dreamed our city

and drew until an August downpour washed it clean. We still
dreamed another chance, a new, more perfect city.

But weather grew unpredictable. My mother told me
not to visit your house and one morning

as the red teakettle screamed, she said you were leaving.
In September, the "For Sale" sign

swung every day in your yard, among the whisking
leaves. One day I saw you outside, packing

a yellow van. I stood quiet. I felt leaves in my throat. It happened
when I lifted my hand in the wind.

I opened my palm. I tried to smile as you faced me then turned
into the open door behind you.

2

That year, my hand felt that wave in every book closed, window locked,
envelope sealed.

Years later, I thought I could taste my fate in the way a lover's lips
would break from mine. I learned

the graceful shoulder turn, thoughtful handshake, one-arm embrace.
I mastered the benign art

of losing numbers, forgetting faces. I practiced the regrettable cough,
hand over chest, and the kindly, "I would love to but,"

the *see you later and yes we'll have to soon*. What you don't know:
the day after you left I found the tracks

of your van. I stepped on them and crushed their muddy furrows,
followed those tracks

as far as I could see and dreamed our city back. Like you, when I left,
I left for good,

to a city of imperfect offices, familiar corridors, doors that swing
open to sidewalks.

3

Where I stand today, the rain begins gently. It grazes my face.
At the crosswalk,

I wait for the light to turn. A woman dressed in black runs to me,
calls me a name I don't know.

She comes to me from a different world. She speaks
a language I've never heard.

When I lift my cap, she sees my strange face, her mistake. She lifts a bashful hand.

The light turns. She whirls her black umbrella into a line of moving faces. I step into my eleventh winter.

Migration

the city
opens its mouth
to me the jaws
of its freeways
its buildings rise
the teeth
of a kind
beast

leaves
fall over
my father's orchard
after harvest he waves
his rake in the air
paves a path back
to the house where
he settles in
for winter

the city
opens its mouth
to me i taste
the peach
i picked the day
i drove away
its meat and pit
still on my tongue

The Flames

for my father

How many nights must it take
one such as me to learn
that we aren't, after all, made
from that bird that flies out of its ashes,
that for a man
as he goes up in flames, his one work
is
to open himself, to be
the flames?
—Galway Kinnell

1

You lift your oxygen mask to ask if I see a dead pigeon
on the burnt loam

and when I shake my head, you stare cold into hospital
light and say

that once your eleven-year-old hands caught a pigeon, held
its body down and sliced

wings from thorax, then left the bird to wrench on red ground.
When you held the trophy wings

to the boys who dared you, the crowd cheered, another boy
lit a match to the pigeon's

body and you stood still holding those wings in the smolder.
How everyone wanted

to be your friend. You tell the story in small breaths,
how no one knew

you cried yourself to sleep for three weeks and you were glad

35

when the rains came,

took to your room and glued model airplanes.

2

As you sunk back into the gurney's buckle, I listened to your staggered
breath, pictured each lung

a vessel of black snowflakes, an envelope containing a sentence
from the hell you could not excavate

but I asked you to breathe the black ash out and as we breathed
into that antiseptic night,

you said you could see your breath smolder, began to cough the rattle
from your chest

until morning when your fever broke, when the nurse brought me
coffee and said, *Happy New Year,*

took you for your morning walk, and I was a child again running down
the empty street,

a filament of blue confetti at my feet.

3
In April we don't speak of December, and you say you have
no memory of that night.

I don't mention your story, don't ask if it's true, don't beg for proof
today in the garden where a pigeon sweeps

down to eat a crumb and as April makes me forget the scars of
December, I throw a piece of bread and see you

stare as I stoop to peer into the nervous fidget of the pigeon's eye.

Seven Days in Intensive Care

It's like this:
you cross
the rope bridge
and the planks
sway with
your every
step

you think
for a moment
you may fall
in the river

think again
and reach
a new side.

Mended

All the long exhale home, my father touches
the new scar on his chest as he watches
the hospital grow small in the rearview mirror.
Then home there are cards and gifts and
friends carrying cakes. My mother makes
another pot of coffee. My father lifts
his hand as he begins to laugh again.
Now the scar is just a signature
of the surgeon's fix. The hospital falls,
a deck of cards, shuffled flat. Days
like these, I want to believe
what mends won't open again
as I stare outside at the river,
watch knives of frenzied currents
rush beneath benign ripples.
Last summer, when a man I loved
years ago stood at my doorstep
I could only hide behind
my yellow curtain, sit and count
the mars and scratches across
my kitchen table. I could only
curl, knees to chest, and wait
for his footsteps to move fainter.
Those steps carried a current, drew
a signature, opened a scar too raw to touch.

Are You

forgetting syllables of honey
and pale Sundays

forgetting your bow against the lips
of a cello

forgetting its pitch ringing to me
in perfect fifths

forgetting the day I slipped down
the marble lane

forgetting I was a kite in wind
rising in my cotton shift

forgetting you crushed
the spider

with your sensible shoe only to find it
biting up your thigh?

Kept

I keep a row of old coats in my back closet. I can't say why. I haven't worn them in years. Maybe someday in an unexpected rain I can offer them to a lost traveler, though a lost traveler has yet to knock on my door.

I keep a row of teacups in my kitchen cabinet. I can't say why. I haven't sipped from them in years. Maybe someday I can offer them to a party of thirsty neighbors, though thirsty neighbors rarely knock on my door.

I keep playing the same movie. I already know the story so I keep the sound down. A girl and boy stand in the snow near a boarding train. The girl hands the boy her ring. The boy clenches his palm. The girl cries as the boy turns and walks down the platform. I know why I watch this. The girl is wearing my coat, one of the coats I keep in my back closet. And as I watch her board the train and take a window seat, I wish she would stop crying but she won't. She takes a hankie from the coat pocket, wipes her face and lets it crumble like a promise. There are buttons on the pockets. There's still snow on the lapels. A porter offers a cup of tea. She takes a sip and for a moment stops weeping. She stares out the window. The movie credits run and I see the slow train descend a white mountain on its way to a distant city. Then I see her again, her face against the window. She's still wearing my coat.

There

You wear an address on your left hand. You keep a gold key in your right. You let him take you to the home you've never seen before. You let him take you, drive you into the city because you love him though you won't say so. You trust him to read the address that you wear on your hand as he drives you over the summer highway. You trust him as he turns onto a lane lined with poplars reciting the numbers of houses. He finds the address you wear on your hand in the gray Victorian with a deep blue door. He says this is the address that you wear on your hand as he stops the car. You tell him this is where you belong, even though you've never been here before. And as he touches your shoulder and says good-bye, you wonder if he may love you too but is afraid to say so. You hold him for a moment because you know you won't see him again now that you have found the address that you wear on you hand. You don't tell him so. As you climb the white steps to the home you've never seen before, you turn to wave one last time. You turn the golden key which fits through the blue door that opens as you hear him drive away.

Missed

Memory is a missing shoe in a frostbitten city. Someone changed
the exits on the interstate. You enter

an anonymous lane. In the distance, a white house with blue shutters.
No one knows

you love the boy who cries in the house down the lane. Tonight you miss
the turn that would lead you to him.

Ice on the shutters. Frost on the lane. Roads close because of weather.
No one hears the cry.

Memory's illustration of night as frostbitten city: misery is a missing
shoe off the shoulder

of the interstate, down a frozen lane, outside a white house. Shuttered.
In a frostbitten city. One lonesome foot.

Crossed

I begin to forget your face.
It grows fainter
as you abridge each
question and answer.

I drifted the floating
branches to the shore,
stood in the vertigo
of inner stairwells,

felt my feet cross the river's
constant relief.

Stitches

NEEDLE

Coraggio, the mother told her daughter. *If you travel with the proper sharpness of angle, you will dance across the most peri-lous crevice.*

THREAD

Who weaves a needle knows the violence of mending. With the right slant, the hand finds a way, a rhythm. All mad repetition creates pattern in motion, anatomy of memory. The tearing and pulling taut, piercing and binding.

SLIPSTITCH

Wrist turns and needle winks as the thread connects across the quarter-inch fold, anchors past tense to pres-ent continuous.

On the other side, all mending is hidden. The fabric ap-pears whole as though nothing were ever separate or broken. If you stare long enough, you begin to believe.

QUESTION

Is the woven always holy?

SCAR

A woman lifts her lover's shirt. Across his chest, she moves her finger to it, touches the edges. Its stitched lips live between what is healed and what will never heal. When she draws her finger from it, threads shrink and rest. Still and resilient. This skin.

Potion

i lifted   your lost words   from the well

handed them back to you

               and they tasted of

                    emerald city apples   these things

good witches   grew like me   born from a falling tree

then i covered you   with silk blankets   when you swaddled

          in poppy sleep   gestated   ontological fires

as you watched me

    melt into water
          that saccharine fog   you called intellect

i woke you

     from my feathery skin

          breathed you

back   into the clever air   this because i am

your potion   i cross my wands   and weave you

more apples   and you will wear

this fruitful amulet

        protection

                from the wizard

who smells the rot   the wound   such wells are born

from any gray   tornado   dream.

Transubstantiation

[Saint Francis and Saint Claire]

> *Love does not exist in and of itself*
> *as a substance: it is the accident of substance.*
> —Dante

1

In the ciborium, the body.

2

Friars carry torches. Flames and shadows
of flames swim along the chapel walls.

3

Light spills onto them at the altar, where she bows
her head, stares into the planks of the floor. She offers
her hair forward, offers because she wants
him to touch her, even if only her
scalp, even if only, his blade.

4

He lifts his hand, tenses his arm in hesitation.

5

The light trembles, turns and shrinks from the torch fires to the ciborium
and then bends into the bowl of holy water. Her strands ignite and glow
as white flames, burning autumn stalks.

6

He lowers his blade into the brightness, lifts the strands and begins
to cut. The threads of her hair fall and recoil still
glowing.

7
Beyond the altar, they are one
flat shadow, the body
to offer.

In November

Out my window, the eucalyptus
holds, in the middle of the yellow
field, a burnt offering to a god
who has gone on winter vacation.
I still pray for April, have faith
in the leaf dream, the bud
that breaks from nothing
but the intention of opening.

The Silence

You laugh when I say my friend grew up
with a ghost

in her parents' house. The whole family knew:
the flickering lights, upset linens,

the small woman shape on the balcony, looking
for someone she'd left behind.

You could feel her, my friend lifted
her hand, said she knew

when a spirit was near, *could tell from the texture
in the air.*

I never believed her stories but still cringed
when dorm lights flickered

early mornings as we walked out to swim.
She disappeared

the next year. Some said she eloped with a soldier.
I never saw her again

but think of her when you say you can't believe
in the unseen.

Yesterday I felt a stir in our house as I looked out
the window to the open field, our refuge

for wounded birds. I tasted the fragrance
of an approaching storm,

felt something enter with the cold air.
It was whole and alive,

a body, pressing us apart, this viscous space
between us,

this violent quiet no sound could shatter,
this unwelcomed guest

insistent on spending the night. I tried to forget,
as I stood in the kitchen

and cut the last summer squash, stopped for a moment
to touch my grazed finger

and watch you read your book by the fire. You turned
a sharp page.

Love, in this silence, how was I to know—
it was your finger that bled.

Adoption

Babies from Romania, girls from China, boys
from Ethiopia. We shuffle through
the pamphlets of faces and

how do you choose, how don't you say,
Yes, we have room for one more. Then
I see the silent question

in your face. As you hold the place, just below
your chest, a space that honors
three dark marks,

a stained path to guide lines of radiation,
the place I can't know
or touch. You

travel into the place they cut and seared, then
sewed shut so you can say
it's over when, of course,

it's never over. In these moments, I see you back
in the garden your father's last summer
as you helped him

walk a brick path lined with irises. You told me
how that day you held his shoulder
and felt the years

of anger scatter into air. How that night in a dream
you ran to catch him
from falling

only to find, on the ground, a small boy

too young to speak, crying over
a skinned knee.

In the Angle of Departure

I believed even the least
light could flood darkness.
Once a stream of fireflies
led me off a broken
highway. I believed
in the map's veracity,
destination's promise,
the window's candle
whispering me home.

Now you tell me that home
is just a stony cavern
at the edge of a desert.
Together we drive
the "Loneliest Road
in America." Obsidian
mountains loom over
monstrous wings of ravens
that cross our path.

Tonight we enter
the blackening desert.
Our headlights are useless
against this thick
shadow ache. It's too late
to turn back. You push
the pedal down. We drive
into the eye of the raven
and fly blind.

Field

The word isn't measured
in letters, only in its weight
against silence.

Throw a pebble into the river.
For how long will the ripples
upset the waves?

If the earth is erased
tomorrow, what will happen
to the moon?

III

*One must always maintain one's connection to the past
and yet ceaselessly pull away from it.*

*It is better to live in a state of impermanence
than in a state of finality.*

—Gaston Bachelard

Listen

Carl bought a peace flag and hung it from his porch. He talked to us across the fence when we gardened and listened to Dylan. Carl liked to sing "Blowin' in the Wind." He hated Vietnam, said it was worse than cancer. He was afraid it would happen again. We sang with Carl. We bought a peace flag. We hung it from our front porch. Another neighbor bought one and there were three. Soon the flags lined our street. At night we lit candles and placed them in windows and prayed that it wouldn't happen again. The war came anyway. A futile silence grew over the neighborhood. One day I saw Carl take his flag down. Others did the same. Carl didn't visit our garden, not even when we played Dylan. Time passed. My daughter felt the new baby kick through my maternity dress. One day Carl picked a bunch of violets from his garden and gave them to her, told me the cancer had come back. Carl died in May. I lost the baby in June. We stopped singing in the garden. We breathed the silence that swept through the neighborhood. The city built a cell tower in the park across the street. It stands five stories above the jungle gym and sandbox. Now the children don't play. The war continues. If you stop by, you'll see the last peace flag wave from our front porch. See its faded canvas, frayed lines. If you walk around back, you can lie in our hammock. Let this book fall from your lap. Listen to the evening garage doors open and close. Let them lull you. After dusk, you might become the silence. If you stay long enough, you may forget to feel yourself breathe.

Summer after His Death

1

The more the peach grew, the more it wanted to break away from the slanted limb. At first she cursed gravity for the constant falling, then she gathered the fruit in her basket.

2

Because it wasn't enough to love the knife, the silver precision, stoic cut, she had to also love the flimsy skin that shriveled back in her hands, the scent of perfect fruit, its dripping meat against her fingers. She loved every fiber she split, the sound of the tearing to the pit, that shrunken fossil heart, petrified blossom.

3

She added sugar to water. Her wooden spoon unraveled a white string of beads, dissolved with a pivot of wrist. If the dead could sing, their voices would rise from liquid.

She added slices of peaches. Syrup thickened, pulled the spoon into folding water. Thought's viscosity. Memory's temperature. Her wrist ached, but her hand was still able. Her voice sang prayers into the mouths of mason jars.

4

She filled the jars. Pushed the lids down. Turned them shut. Pieces of fruit coalesced with syrup, then cooled. Phantoms on the window turned to water. Cold lines running. Memory's temperature. The ache in the wrist, the arm. These days. These hours. At times, even breath aches.

5

Afternoon deepens. Stars from her hands, still carrying specks of sugar, echo from the lamppost outside her window, where a breeze shifts through a break in glass, cancels the breath of her last sigh. Stillness in the room without.

A Tide

It begins after the crash, after
the smell of grease, the pop
of glass, after her car caroms
embankment to levee, one
wheel still spinning. When her life
is an eyelash flutter away
from the river, that's when she breaks
from the half-opened
door, screams to the black
morning and crawls
to the ground, worms her way
through mud and climbs the bank.
Each fall breeds
a shadow. Each shadow breeds
rage, until she scales the riverbank, grabs
the stalks of weeds
with bloodied hands, and stands
again for the first time, learns
again to balance on two legs.
Now she blots the blood
from her hands on her torn skirt
and steps up to the road, moving
toward town, where later you will see her
clean, bandaged, waving hello.
And you will notice something,
a wilderness in her eyes, an animal
in her gait. But now she is limping,
not waiting for the sirens, the wheel
still spinning inside her.
And her walk steadies as day
takes shape. A vein
of light scales the riverbank
through the crook in the road

and her eyes open to a wave
of blue air, transparent.

The Night Held Them

The happy family dancing around the bonfire. Halloween party. Mother holding the laughing baby in her bee suit. Father singing and clapping beside them. And the night held them through the dark drive home. Baby sleeping in the backseat. Mother and father watching the headlights split laces of fog. The night held them as they approached the stoplight, where they heard a thousand vials breaking. When they saw, in the distance, a car burn into a tree. When they asked, *What to do? What to do?* When a man yelled, *Stay back.* When they sat and watched the spitting blaze, the night anchored them. In the air they tasted dark water. It's the water a swimmer fears, when someone is drowning. It's the water beneath the wriggling feet, where she dives and kicks but can't creep deep enough. It's the blood of a wound the surgeon must probe to find the source of pain. When does he stop his scalpel? Where does he place the consoling stitch? *What to do?* And the mother whispers, *Whose child?* She never met the young marine on leave for a week, dressed as a prince, driving to a party. Five miles away, moonlight falls on a chessboard. A woman waiting in a window adjusts her tiara. She says, *He should be here.* They move on: the cars that collect at the light. The patrolman swings his flair like a lantern, guiding them across. And the night held the family as the father drove forward. As the mother turned back, her finger touching the baby's candy bracelet. Sirens in the distance. Too late. The father saying, *What could we have done?* The mother watching the way the flames from the blaze flicker across the baby's face, light her bee wings and hat. And the baby releasing a dreamy chuckle, sleeping through it all.

The Dance

The mother puts the tea
kettle on the stove, mixes
the breakfast biscuits as
the baby dances with tele
vision elmo, and the tele
phone rings as the kettle
screams as the doctor says
hello, your breast biopsy
and the mother takes the
kettle from the stove as the
doctor says *benign*
everything fine and the
mother says, *benign*
thank you, yes
and *how was your thanks*
giving, fine she says
and *thank you* and
the mother puts the
biscuits in the oven
rinses a cluster of
grapes, lets the water
fall over every purple
bulb as the baby
babbles with tele
vision elmo and she
dances and she
dances and the mother
pours herself
a cup of tea.

In a Distant Country

I watch the evening news. The anchorman says someone suffers
in a distant country. Outside my window

a cat chases a rabbit through the yard. I hear a cry. It echoes
through my skin. Outside I expect to find something

wounded or dead. I don't. Behind the tomato plants, over
the fence, I search but see nothing.

I hear notes play from a distant piano, smell bread bake in the house
next door. I still feel the cry

chill my skin. Something near me suffers. I can do nothing but stand
in the middle of my garden

and watch the shadow of summer's hand close in, the darkness
coming quicker, over my

picture window. The room as I left it. My body's impression remains
on the chair. My half-eaten dinner

on the tray. There the anchorman says someone suffers in another
distant country. He speaks to an empty room.

Photograph in a Window

1

They stand in an unexpected snowstorm. My mother wears his coat
over her paisley dress.

My father's arm bows around her shoulder. They are laughing.
Strange day.

Hardly ever snows so far below the Sierra. In the distance, their future
takes shape in a house near the river.

Not yet built, but beginning. A slab of concrete, a few beams
of fresh lumber.

I hold this picture, waiting to be conceived in the house by the river,
to be born in an unexpected gust of weather.

2

I stand in another house that overlooks a field.
Tomorrow's trucks will turn this field

and level hills, make way for new slabs of concrete. I will leave this
house, this field,

for a new house down a well-paved street.

3

I want to hold this field like a photograph in my mind.
Nine white petals spiraling

against the grass, the astringent twigs of eucalyptus. I want to see
everything, as I see this field.

Yet a crooked line of yellow history winks in the edges
of the photograph I lift

from the windowsill, hold in my hands. My mother grew to hate
the house near the river

where I ran through sprinklers and climbed trunks of walnut trees.
We left that house empty

and moved into town where my father dreamed of rivers
and refused to mow the lawn.

4

I will wrap this photograph in paper and soft fabric. I will kiss
the field for the last time.

I will take them with me. Somewhere beyond the photograph's
edges, a lumber truck turns

a slow right in an unexpected gust of snow. I will be born.
Down a well-paved street,

I will hear a wind's rasp as it combs the field's weeds.

Because He Feared the Call to Vietnam

It begins with a leak in the kitchen sink.

It begins with father's foot tapping in 6/8 time. It begins
with mother cutting the overcooked roast

and child stabbing a thumb through the navel of an orange.

Then mother tears each page of her *Betty Crocker Cookbook*
in two when father breaks mother's vase

as child tears the skin of an orange

and mother viciously sweeps the kitchen floor as father
hits the television for not talking . . .

It ends with a finch hitting the window.

It ends with mother rubbing her eyes with Kleenex, then walking
outside to wipe a drop of blood

from the glass. It ends with father lighting a cigarette and watching
television without sound.

It ends as I listen to a leak in the kitchen sink

and suck the pulp of an orange dry.

Body in Translation

When I saw my body
young and pregnant,
lying in a casket—

I screamed, *there must be*
a mistake. Look at her
ruddy skin—

See this body
breathe.

My neighbor strikes
a hammer against
his fence—

I wake and stand
before a mirror.
See this body

breathe through
worn elastic
alphabets,

hear this year's syllables
harder than
the last's.

A hammer strikes
against a fence.

Outside my window,
gusts tear
an open field.

The geese flock
here—

against the
storm
then turn

to catch
the wind.

Summer of Mirrors

Think of the secret and its price. Two girls chase waves
on a sandy beach.
A mother calls

one girl away. She offers her friend a silver charm
before she runs.
The other girl

takes the charm and waits for her friend
to return. Still alone, on the last
day of summer

she throws the charm from the boardwalk.
Why keep what you don't need?
This summer

I open closets, empty boxes, lift clothes
from racks.
I carry out

white plastic bags and wait for the truck
to take them. The more I give away
the sweeter I feel.

Now that I've taken the sweaters from under the bed,
I turn lighter to the night.
In my dreams

I see reflections of past faces move on a swift river.
I believe they
still sing.

Estate Sale

The door opens and they march
in to seize something they don't
know they need and it doesn't
matter the house still smells
of the dead woman's perfume
her son and daughter sit in
the corner and watch them
rake and stack ask how much
and how much less and the son
feels sick as the lady in the other
corner puts on his mother's hat
then he eyes a young couple
as they look at the sturdy old
dresser the man has a hole
in his overcoat the woman puts
her arms around him as the
son walks to them and says
you can have it and they smile
and admire it but the man
with the hole in his overcoat
insists on giving some-
thing and the woman nods
but the son says no you
can have it let me help you
pack it and he carries
it out to fit into the trunk
of the small blue Honda and
the son goes back for rope
then knits the dresser to
the trunk and they shake hands
as the couple says thank you
and more people flood into
the house as the couple
fumble into their old

weighed-down car and
they wave as they leave
with the sturdy old dresser
in the jaws of their
trunk and they take it
with them and they take
it with them.

Why the Kiss Good-bye

Don't ask why I walked
through one last time.
Now the empty house.
After I'd swaddled
the last china cups
in blue-fringed hankies
and carried them away.
Don't ask why I wanted
to walk into the empty,
feel my feet creak against
the hardwood floors.
Why I leaned against
bare lemonade walls
and listened to the kitchen
faucet drip. Don't ask
why I cruised the hallway
like when I was six.
Why one last stare
at the breaking fence
outside the bedroom window.
Why clip a piece of thread
from the withering drape.
Why one last smell of yellow
linen closet. Why one more
thumbprint against a crack
in the bathroom mirror.
Why make the new owners
wait in the rain with their saws
and toolboxes. Why open
the slow door. Why hesitate
to take key from ring and say
Here now it's yours.
Why walk away to the rhythm
of faucet drip. Why hear it

again in the rain. Why open
my mouth and let a raindrop
hit, its weight so cold
against my teeth.

Carnival

Today I walk by the vendors on the corner. They stand
in sequined suits.

They speak through plastic teeth. I hear hunger in their voices
as I clutch my purse and hurry past.

When I was seven I fed a lizard an old piece of lettuce
and as I watched his jaws

clamp the rusty leaf, I knew this appetite was mine.
At the church carnival

I told the nuns I wanted no part of a heaven that didn't allow
animals through the gates.

Sister Nicolausala hugged me and whispered, *If you want animals
in heaven, you will have them.*

She walked me to the prize wheel. I placed a dime on number five
and when the wheel stopped at six,

Sister slid the dime over and said, *You win.* The man behind the booth
handed me a stuffed bumblebee.

I pulled Sister's habit and shook my head. She said,
Take it and don't ask why.

She walked away and my friends gathered to knit their hands
around my bee and say, *You're so lucky.*

We rustled to the ringtoss, fishbowl, tic-tac-toe. That day
I ran to win every game I played.

Visitation

It took two days to drive through the desert, a week before I began
to see green again. The first time I saw my son, he was

five years old, sitting at my kitchen table, staring at cartooned faces
on a cereal box. He smiled

with a full set of milk teeth, said he knew I'd been waiting to see his
chestnut hair, his strong chin that favored my grandfather's.

He cupped his hands around the fruit bowl, then softly grazed his finger
against an apricot skin.

He never said why he wasn't born like his sister, who heaved breaths on
my belly, fluttered her eyes and twitched her lips

open as they sweetly cut the cord. But he slipped behind the burgundy
curtain, asked me to play hide-and-seek.

I turned around and said that summer it took two days to drive through
the desert.

I turned back and opened the burgundy curtain, faced an empty
window, pressed my hands into frozen glass.

Your Birthday That Was Not

is an empty white
calendar square
though I rise from bed
heavy as though you
were with me.

As a child, I dreamed
that I woke floating
in a still, warm ocean.
Then I swam toward
an island that I could
not reach. My arms,
turning the water over,
loved this swimming
without ending, opening
into waking, shadows
on the window, arms
limp at my sides.

Once I thought
if I were still
you would not fall
away from me.
Now when I look
at the clouds
I feel you moving
away, no matter
where I stand.

Every day when I wake
and wash my face, I feel
my body turning
away from you.

I scribble on a blank
page, still turning
to feel you, alive
in every error.

Familiar Rhymes

An entire past comes to dwell in a new house.
—Gaston Bachelard

The moving van packed outside the house, cupboards emptied,
and my daughter refuses

to go to bed. She says, *I won't leave. You will have to move without me.*
Hands on hips.

Nostrils flaring. High-pitched sobs when we carry her down
the porch steps. Weeks later

she sits in our foreign kitchen, pouring syrup over pancakes and says,
OK. I'll stay here a while, but this is not my home.

She says when she's older, she'll babysit, save money and buy
the old house back.

Some nights she wakes and says she's been back in the garden finding
snails in the grass, holding them and watching

their slick bodies curl in an out of shells. Other nights she wakes to say
she has met her unborn

sister and brother climbing the old eucalyptus. Sometimes I picture her
at eighteen reading Plato,

contemplating other homes the mind holds and forgiving us
for carrying her here.

Now the doorbell rings and the neighbor girls ask her to play. She leaves
and follows them

down the sidewalk. As I wash syrup from her plate, I hear the sound
of girls skipping rope.

Rhythms of woven twine hitting the driveway next door.
Familiar rhymes in new voices.

Gift

One must imagine Sisyphus happy.
—Camus

When my daughter finds
a one-winged ladybug
crawling in the gravel
she carries its torn body
down the driveway to find
the perfect leafy home.

I don't tell her I've been
watching all along from
the window as I wrap
a present for my friend
coming home from
the hospital again.

I draped the gift
in ribbons, opened
my scissors like a dagger
and curled the strands
around my blade
until they spiraled
out of my hands.

When my daughter calls
from the garden,
I walk out to find
her ladybug
trying to climb
a safe leaf,
lifting its wing.

A Careful Angle

beginning with a line from Tomas Tranströmer

The morning air delivers its letters
with stamps that glow.

The children love the light and dust
that seeps through the mail slot.

Some days your truths are shoes
that won't fit:

so unlike the message that lies
in your doorway.

There's a technique to opening
another address,

a careful angle by which you unveil.

After Three Years, I Open My Briefcase

I brushed the dust away,
wiped it clean

and soon it looked
new again

though heavier it seemed
tugging my arm.

Leaving the house,
I rediscovered

the low hum of morning freeways,
the florescence

of offices, smells of coffee and ink,
fluttering sounds

of keyboard fingers, cubicle
whispers.

It was like I had never been
gone at all.

I was walking in
after a weekend,

waking from a short nap.
But as I sat

at my new desk and opened
the old briefcase—

I remembered a story
about the monk

who made one thousand perfect bowls,
for it was his vocation

each day, to spin clay against
his fingers,

feel the prayerful angles
of his palms,

the precision of each finish
more flawless

than the last. And the day
he spun

the thousandth bowl,
quietly

his teacher walked through
to see.

He said, *These are the finest*
I've seen. You've nearly

found your vocation.
Then he offered

the silver staff
and the monk

accepted the weight of his gift.
The teacher whispered

as he gently placed the staff
in the monk's hand—

Now break each bowl
and begin again . . .

Beatific

Who knows, but that the universe is not one vast sea of compassion actually,
the veritable holy honey, beneath all this show
of personality and cruelty?
—Jack Kerouac

There you can hear a child cough in a canyon. There you can see
her sweatshop awl bore your coat buttons.

There you can hold her calloused hands. There you can taste
the hobo's bourbon and the blood on his broken dog's claw.

There you can listen to the beaten child stutter all the languages
you've never heard.

But you can't stay there long, for fear you may dissolve.
So you come here and lock your doors,

for there may come knocking. And it's better here
everyone knows,

here where sweet plums grow outside your window.
Here you can have meringues and tea

and read old books and dream in your comfortable chair
though you know there lives just outside

your eye's corner. Today you go back and stand three steps
over border.

If you listen beyond the siren sounds and beggars' pleas,
you hear harmonies of choirs that light a sky on fire.

Then you know there must be closer to heaven.
There where it's always

winter, you button your coat and the girl from the sweatshop smiles
because she thought

she'd never see you again. There where a hungry woman
offers

a piece of bread you won't take because you're turning back here.
There where you find a book in your pocket.

There where you turn the first page and know it wasn't written here
in a comfortable chair.

There where you feel the poet's pulse rush from the other side
of the page.

Notes

"Found": This poem imitates syntactical patterns in Robert Bly's translation of Tomas Tranströmer's poem "Tracks."

"A Careful Angle": Words in italics are from Robin Fulton's translation of Tranströmer's "Noon Thaw," in Tomas Tranströmer, *The Great Enigma: New Collected Poems*, trans. Robin Fulton (New York: New Directions, 2006).

"Dream in a Forgotten Language": Words in italics are phrases from Gertrude Stein's essay "Composition as Explanation," in *Selected Writings of Gertrude Stein*, ed. Carl Van Vechten (New York: Vintage, 1990).

"Listen": This poem is written in memory of Carl Courtier.

"The Silence," "Adoption" and "In the Angle of Departure": These poems are for Thomas Gillaspy.

The quotation "One must always maintain one's connection to the past and then ceaselessly pull away from it" is from Gaston Bachelard, *Fragments of a Poetics of Fire*, trans. Kenneth Haltman (Dallas: Dallas Institute, 1990).

All other Bachelard quotations are from his *The Poetics of Space*, trans. by Maria Jolas (Boston: Beacon, 1964).

Quotations from Italo Calvino are from *Invisible Cities,*
trans. by William Weaver (New York: Harcourt, 1974).

About the Author

Marcene Gandolfo's work has appeared in several literary journals, including *DMQ Review, Bayou, Poet Lore, Harpur Palate, Van Gogh's Ear, The Café Review, Red Rock Review,* and *Paterson Literary Review.* She teaches writing and literature at Sacramento City College and lives in Elk Grove, California, with her husband, daughter, and three cats.

CPSIA information can be obtained at www.ICGtesting.com
Printed in the USA
BVOW07s1028200114

342328BV00003B/6/P